EU GDPR compliance compact: GDPR Checklist and GDPR Introduction for Websites and Bloggers

GDPR handbook with GDPR templates. Data Protection Regulation 2018 for beginners. GDPR concisely explained

Table of Contents

1. Data Protection, Data Security & GDPR

The Data Protection Regulation (GDPR) concerns all of us. Whether you a blogger, website operator, shop owner or a company. It does not matter if you are working online or offline. It is important that you deal with this topic.

In forums and on social media it is repeatedly heard "I don't have time for the GDPR", "I don't do anything", "I am waiting". As an entrepreneur, this is grossly negligent, to wait and see where the most things are not new and has been valid for years.

Another important note:

"I point out that this is not a legal advice. If you have any questions, please contact a lawyer in this field. He can offer expert advice. Likewise, an appropriate consultant or specialist lawyer should be consulted for individual advice. "

Most of the links are in German. You can translate them with the google translator Plugin / Web browser plugin, if you are interested in the source links.

Anyone who works in online marketing or generally on the Internet and thus collects or even processes data in any form, should not only have heard of this, but must deal with it. This, because, the whole business is based on and is dependent on "data protection, data security and GDPR".

But first, what's the difference between privacy and data security? Here are some definitions:

Data protection is about protecting the privacy of every person. Data protection guarantees every citizen a right to informational self-determination and protects him or her against the misuse of his or her data. For the processing of personal data, there are rules that are laid down in the BDSG or the data protection laws of the countries. Here, you have to ask whether personal data may be processed at all. **Source see footnote**[1]

Personal data pursuant to section 3 paragraph 1 BDSG is "Individual details about personal or factual circumstances of a specific or specifiable natural person". Source see footnote[2]

[1]   Vgl.   https://www.datenschutzbeauftragter-info.de/unterschiede-zwischen-datenschutz-datensicherheit-informationssicherheit-oder-it-sicherheit/

Data security should address security risks and protect the data against manipulation, loss or unauthorized access. So, here is not the question of whether data may be collected and processed at all (that is a question of data protection), but the question of what measures must be taken to protect the data. Data security must be ensured in the context of data protection in accordance with section 9 BDSG (including the annex) by implementing suitable technical and organizational measures. Source see footnote [3]

So that means that you are responsible for privacy and data security of the data. You have to ensure that the data - especially the personal data - is protected for your visitors and customers.

This is especially so if you collect e-mail addresses and use tracking tools like Google Analytics, Matomo or others. Here you should make sure that what you use is data protection compliant. This means you must sign a contract with Google Analytics and submit it in duplicate to Google Ireland Ltd.

You also have to choose your settings so that the IP addresses

[2] Vgl. https://www.gesetze-im-internet.de/bdsg_1990/__3.html

[3]   Vgl.   https://www.datenschutzbeauftragter-info.de/unterschiede-zwischen-datenschutz-datensicherheit-informationssicherheit-oder-it-sicherheit/

of the respective visitors are anonymized, that is, in Google Analytics, check the option "anonymize IP". Of course, this also applies to any other tracking tool that you use.

You also have to pay attention to the social media buttons, as they can only be used if a connection will be only established when the user clicks on this button. Permanent tracking is therefore not allowed.

From May 25, 2018, the GDPR is complete, that is, the transition period of two years is over and now everyone has to comply. Whether you live in the EU or just provide a service in the EU which uses and processes the data of EU citizens. If you do not abide by it, **you have to expect fines of up to 4% of the company's worldwide turnover or up to 20 million euros**.

When collecting e-mail addresses, of course, you must ensure that you use the Double-Opt-In variant. This means that if someone signs up in your newsletter, they must first confirm their email address and actively i.e. by typing it out themselves.

When collecting e-mail addresses, of course, you must ensure that you use the Double-Opt-In variant. This means that if someone signs up in your newsletter, they must first confirm their email address and actively i.e. by typing it out themselves. The user logs in with his data in your newsletter, gets a confirmation email with a confirmation link deposited in the e-mail sent.

Only when the user confirms this link, by clicking on it, is he or she considered a confirmed user and you can then send him or her your newsletter. Otherwise, it is not allowed and you can be prosecuted for it. This applies not only since the coming into force of the GDPR, but also since the BDSG (German law).

Furthermore, with GDPR it is now important that you show the user who gets to your site, which data you collect, how you do it and what you use it for. All this belongs in the subpage "Privacy". Here the users should be able to get more information. This is an important page, next to the imprint. The imprint includes your name and address, e-mail and a telephone number under which you can be reached.

Furthermore, as long as you declare a sales tax, your VAT ID is included. But now further regarding the privacy page. If you use social media such as Facebook, Twitter, etc., you must also list this here. The same applies if you participate in Amazon's affiliate program.

E-recht24 offers a good and free generator for imprint and data protection.[4] The Premium Account is recommended[5], due to additional tools and extended privacy policy. There is also a template for joining the Amazon Affiliate Program as provided by Flegl Lawyers.[6]

You have to, if you collect data and you will do when someone visits your website (IP address) also create a processing directory. This is a documentation or spreadsheet that lists what you collect, how they are used, who are allowed to use it, and whether they leave the EU.

In addition, you must specify how long they are stored and when they are deleted, that is, the deletion deadlines. Information about the technical and organizational measures (TOM) must also be disclosed. Here, for example, it is necessary to know whether you encrypt the files in any way

---

[4] Vgl. https://www.e-recht24.de/impressum-generator.html

[5] Vgl. http://bit.ly/e-recht24-premium-acc*

[6] Vgl. https://www.flegl-rechtsanwaelte.de/muster-datenschutzerklaerung-amazon

or whether you inform the interested parties, customers or partners in writing or by telephone about the collection and use of the data.

When visiting your website, the user should be notified of the use of cookies and have the opportunity to agree, refuse and read more details. For more details, you can usually link to your privacy page. An example of a processing directory can be found at BITKOM.[7]

A responsible person must be designated who will be available in case of requests from the authorities. As a rule, it is the managing director, the owner or operator of the website or the service. For private companies larger than 250 employees, a data protection officer is necessary. Unless particularly risky data is processed.

It is important to note that your solution (website, service, etc.) should already be defined and designed in such a way that it complies with the guidelines of the GDPR, keyword "privacy by default and privacy by design". More about "GDPR" can be found on the official GDPR website.[8]

---

[7] Vgl. https://www.bitkom.org/Bitkom/Publikationen/Das-Verarbeitungsverzeichnis.html

Also, you should check your website to see that there is not too much tracking and spying, or to find out if the plugins that you are using are not allowed because of tracking. You can find a good overview at blogmojo.de[9]. A corresponding checklist can be found in the next chapter.

This was only a small ride into the topic of data protection, data security and the GDPR. These are complex issues and require expert and individual Advice from an expert who can assist with analysis and implementation. At this point, I only wanted to point out the most important things, so that you will have heard about them and are not therefore not fazed with the facts.

After reading this section, you may be a little confused because there are indeed some things that you have to implement and pay attention to. However, if you start, you'll have to pay attention to a few things anyway, so that you can get it right the first time.

---

[8] Vgl. https://www.eugdpr.org/

[9] Vgl. https://www.blogmojo.de/wordpress-plugins-GDPR/

So, you do not need to change or re-document the old stuff. For most things, there are already aids and tools, sometimes even free, so that you can face this hurdle relatively easily. You do not have to be confused, go ahead with your idea and your project.

In the next few chapters, I'd like to split the whole thing into smaller pieces to make it easier and more helpful to grasp.

1.1. GDPR Checklist

This list is intended to help you to keep track of the various to-dos so that you can create or configure your site to conform to the GDPR guidelines.

GDPR and Hosting

Have you completed a contract data processing (CDP) contract with your web hosting provider (s)?[10]	
Does your site use a Content Delivery Network (CDN)?	
If so, is the server in the EU?	
If so, do you have a CDP closed with this provider? (If	

---

[10] https://www.gdd.de/eforen/nuernberg/intern/aktuelle-praxistipps/MustervertragsanlageAuftragsdatenverarbeitung_BITKOM12_091.pdf/

the data is not stored on the web server where your page is running)	
If not, does the provider comply with the guidelines of the GDPR and EU-US Privacy Shield? (Have confirmation sent) (See Chapter 5, Art. 44 GDPR)	

Encoding

Did you install an SSL certificate on your website?	
Is the SSL certificate valid?	
Have you taken any action against unauthorized access by hackers or third parties? (secure file permissions, secure passwords, regular updates, if necessary .htpasswd)	

GDPR Tracking Tools

Do you have a tracking tool in use; Piwik, Matomo, Google Analytics, Wordpress.com stats, Yandex etc.? If yes, which one do you use?	
Did you anonymize the IP addresses? (Google Analytics, Piwik / Matomo)	
If Google Analytics, would it be possible to switch to Piwik, or, Matomo? With own server?	
Is the data on your server? Or the third party?	
If third party, is this in the EU?	

If so, is this in Germany?	
Did you complete a CDP with this?	
If outside the EU, do you have a way to change it?	
If not, does the provider comply with the GDPR and EU-US Privacy Shield guidelines? (Have confirmation sent) (See Chapter 5, Art. 44 GDPR)	
Can the user object to the capture by one click? (Link should be in the privacy policy)	

Forms

Are forms embedded on your website that transfer personal data? (without HTTPS you cannot include forms)	
If so, do you have any hints regarding the use of the data? (below, above, next, in short form)	
Is there a reference to your privacy policy?	

Newsletter in the General Data Protection Regulation

Is a newsletter plugin or service used?	
Is it ensured that the use of the newsletter plug-in or service and thus the registration of the user in the newsletter is according to the double-opt-in procedure? (Double-Opt-In = entry in the newsletter	

and subsequent confirmation of the e-mail address by e-mail).	
Is there an indication regarding the use of the data?	
Are you collecting all the email addresses on your page together in one pot?	
If so, did you alert the user that he could also receive other information and, if appropriate, offers, by signing up for the newsletter?	
If you use a plugin: is the data stored on your server?	
If you use a service provider: is it in the EU?	
If so, do you have a CDP closed with this?	
If not, does the provider comply with the guidelines of the GDPR and EU-US Privacy Shield? (Have confirmation sent) (See Chapter 5, Art. 44 GDPR)	

Plugins, widgets, calculators, iframes, etc.

Do you use plugins, widgets, iframes, scripts or other interfaces on your website?	
Does this save personal data?	
If so, with you on the server?	
Or at a third party?	
For what purpose is the data stored?	
Will only the data needed or possibly too much	

data be stored?	

Membership

Do you use membership functions or services?	
Is the data stored on your server?	
If so, is this server in the EU?	
Did you close a CDP with this hosting provider?	
If the server is outside the EU, does the provider comply with the GDPR and EU-US Privacy Shield guidelines? (Have confirmation sent) (See Chapter 5, Art. 44 GDPR)	

Note: Membership, newsletter, social media, form plugins always collect personal information. The same can also apply to financial computers or other computers and tools where name, address or e-mail address must be entered.

It is best if you read in the respective documentation of the provider or plugin, what is sent and where it goes. Hopefully most of them have already heard about GDPR and adapted their services and documentation accordingly. However, you will also find those who have not heard about it yet and don't have prepared anything or only insufficient. Only one thing helps, you have to find out for yourself which tools collect and send data. You can use the following methods:

- Open Chrome Developer Tools (right click -> Examine -
  > go to "Sources" tab)
- You can also find cookies on Chrome by clicking on the
  "i" or the key symbol in the address bar to the left of the
  domain:

- o A window will pop up showing you the number of
    cookies, where you can click this button and get
    more information as you go along
- For Firefox, too, if you click on the "i" or the key symbol
  in the address bar to the left of the domain:

- o Then a window opens where you have to click on
    the arrow to the right and finally at the bottom on
    "further information" and there on "show cookies".
- You can also use the page "builtwith.com"
- Or you use Ghostery (browser plugin)
  https://www.ghostery.com/de/

Online Shops

Online shops can be structured differently and therefore it is difficult to respond to, as this can be very complex. Especially with credit cards and other data regarding finances, it is very critical regarding data privacy. Fundamental and some topics can still be taken up:

Do you host your shop yourself?	
If not, is the service provider located in the EU?	
If so, did you complete a CDP with him?	
If outside the EU: does the provider comply with the GDPR and EU-US Privacy Shield guidelines? (Have confirmation sent) (See Chapter 5, Art. 44 GDPR)	
Do you use external payment services?	
If so, did you detail in your privacy policy what data will be collected and sent to where?	
Also note here again, CDP agreement with your payment service provider.	
If outside the EU: does the provider comply with the GDPR and EU-US Privacy Shield guidelines? (Have confirmation sent) (See Chapter 5, Art. 44 GDPR)	
Is a package tracking system used?	
Is this email or phone number used?	
Did you mention this in your privacy policy?	

If so, do you have a CDP with this service provider closed?	
If outside the EU: does the provider comply with the GDPR and EU-US Privacy Shield guidelines? (Have confirmation sent) (See Chapter 5, Art. 44 GDPR)	
Does the user need to register to be able to place the order?	
If so, is this marked accordingly?	
Is this also listed in the privacy policy?	
Do you have a secure password (at least 10 digits, lowercase / uppercase, numbers, special characters) for accessing the shop backend?	
Do you have a secure password for the database?	
Are all other passwords used for the shop system also safe?	
Is the connection encrypted? (without SSL no shop)	
Is the IT around the shop (web server, website, network, database, interfaces, etc.) well secured? Here it is necessary that this is thoroughly examined by an IT expert.	
List all your interfaces and external service providers and check if you have a CDP with them (for customer and employee data necessary).	

Also, check if any service providers that come into contact with customer data (but also employee data) are in the EU, otherwise you will need to check if the service provider outside the EU complies with all GDPR regulations.	

Marketing

The topic of marketing is also very complex. This is partly because you do not know which interfaces and systems are still connected to the platform and what might happen behind them. Important for your own site is therefore that you check which interfaces and marketing tools and software is connected, as well as what they do.

A few points:

Do you use Google Analytics or similar?	
If so, did you list this in your privacy policy?	
Do you use DoubleClick?	
If so, did you list this in your privacy policy?	
Do you use Google AdSense or similar?	
If so, did you list this in your privacy policy?	
Are you using the Facebook Pixel or similar?	

If so, did you list this in your privacy policy?	
Do you have a built-in possibility that the user can contradict the tracking?	
Basically, the topic "tracking and marketing" is very sensitive. Therefore, even if it is very unpleasant, it would be better if you include an opt-out method. This allows the user to object to the tracking.	
Especially with the Remarketing / Retargeting options, it is better if you incorporate an opt-in method, so that the user must explicitly agree that he wants to be tracked. Also, that he clicks on the Facebook Like button and then his data are used accordingly.	

Social Media (Plugins)

Do you use social media plugins?	
Did you mention this in your privacy policy?	
If you use the social media plugins, is it ensured that no personal information is transferred before the user can object? (Applies to the standard sharing buttons).	
Use alternative plugins, such as. e.g. the Shariff Plugin (for WordPress)	
Do you use the Affiliatetheme.io? Then the social	

media plugins are already GDPR compliant (they are only links).	
Do you have an imprint on your social media pages or do you at least link to your imprint?	

What is a contract data processing contract (CDP contract)?

Now the word "order data processing" CDP has been used several times already. For the sake of completeness, I would like to briefly explain what that is. If you use the services of web hosts or other service providers, they will process your customers' personal information. In order to ensure the security and protection of the data of these users and customers by the external contractor, for this processing of data by an external contractor, a so-called contract for order data processing (CDP contract) is necessary and have to be closed.

Who needs a contract data processing contract?

Anyone who processes personal information. This means that if you use a service provider or service from an external provider, or if your users' personal information is stored on a server that is not yours, then a CDP contract is required. In many companies, a large amount of data is processed and passed on to external providers, sometimes without having to deal with it or being aware of it. Therefore, it is necessary to check this data transmission and to question whether the data at all have to be transmitted to the external service provider and partner in this level of detail.

In any case, you need a CDP contract here. Above all, it is important that it applies to all service providers and partners in the EU. Service providers outside the EU must comply with the data protection provisions of the General Data Protection Regulation, since otherwise personal data may not be processed there.

A great overview of the various service providers and their contribution to the CDP contract has been created on blogmojo[11]. There you can see which hosters and service providers have already created CDP contracts. You can then download, fill out and send it to the service provider.

What is a privacy policy?

This term also appears more often in the checklist. A privacy policy describes the actions someone takes to protect the privacy of customers, employees or users. Particularly

---

[11] Vgl. https://www.blogmojo.de/CDP-vertraege/ (German)

noteworthy here are the personal data. Creating a privacy policy is mandatory next to the imprint. These can be created through a lawyer, which could be very costly or you can use the free or paid generators on the internet for this.

For example, you can use the following generators:

- Data protection generator of the DGD (German society for data protection, free of charge) [12]

- eRecht24 Data Protection Generator (Premium Account recommended * for more tools and advanced privacy policy) [13]

- Datenschutz-Generator von Dr. Schwenke (free of charge) [14]

What is personal data?

Personal data are defined according to section § 3 Abs. 1 BDSG[15] as individual information on personal or factual circumstances of a particular or identifiable natural person.[16]

---

[12] Vgl. https://www.e-recht24.de/muster-datenschutzerklaerung.html (German)

[13] Vgl. https://www.e-recht24.de/muster-datenschutzerklaerung.html

[14] Vgl. https://datenschutz-generator.de/

[15] Vgl. https://www.gesetze-im-internet.de/bdsg_1990/__3.html

[16] Vgl. https://www.datenschutzbeauftragter-info.de/personenbezogene-daten-definition-und-praktische-beispiele/

That is, personal information is information that can make any personal reference to a person. These include:

- Name and address
- E-mail address
- Phone
- Credit card and bank account information
- Employee Number
- Customer number
- Photo
- Personal description
- License Plate

In addition, there is the "special personal data", which is equivalent to medical information on the person.

1.2. What is a Procedure Directory?

The list of procedures has been constantly discussed in recent weeks and months. People always asked what that was and what they needed. But do not worry, it's often not that bad. The procedure directory is an overview of all procedures and processes used that come into contact with personal data and process it. So, no matter if it's colleagues or employees who come in contact with this data, a procedure directory is needed for these processes and procedures.

It should be noted that it is not just about customer data, but also about user and employee data. For example, payroll and employee administration as well as itemized bill and e-mail list for the newsletter must be classified accordingly and a list of procedures is required.

1.3. Who Needs a Procedure Directory?

In short: EVERYONE! Article 30 of the GDPR "List of processing activities" states that only 250 employees or more need such a directory. However, the same paragraph states that this only applies if the processing is not just occasional. So, if you handle the collected e-mail addresses of newsletter subscribers and send them to e-mails, then this is no longer uncommon. Also, with the employee data and customer data is not only occasionally handled, but regularly. It is questionable here what one sometimes understands.

1.4. What Belongs in a Procedure Directory?

Article 30 of the GDPR "List of processing activities" lists what is in the list of procedures. The following information must be included in the procedure directory:

- Name of the data protection officer (if required)
- Name and contact of the person responsible for the procedure
- WHY (purpose) of processing the data
- Who is affected? (Groups);
- What data is collected from those affected?
- Who has access to this data (internally, externally, outside the EU)
- How does the transfer to the third country (outside the EU) take place?
- Is this transfer legally secured?
- What deletion dates are provided for this data (if provided)
- General technical description of data security (if possible) (= TOM => Technical and organizational measures)

Bitkom has provided an example here or a sample including a guide that can be downloaded and adapted for free. [17].

Also, a very good overview offers Mrs. Regina Stoiber, including explanation and pattern for download.[18]

---

[17] Vgl. https://www.bitkom.org/Bitkom/Publikationen/Das-Verarbeitungsverzeichnis.html

[18] Vgl. https://regina-stoiber.com/2018/03/11/datenschutz-verfahrensverzeichnis-nach-artikel-30-GDPR-mit-muster/

1.5. What Does a Pattern Procedure Directory Look Like?

To create a directory of procedures you can proceed in various ways. In addition to a data protection expert, a special software can be purchased, which creates such a procedure directory with a beautiful interface. But this can also be done easily with Excel. Because the main work remains and is the same, the entry. Because you have to take on this task yourself. You have to go through each procedure and enter it accordingly.

- Name of the data protection officer (if necessary)

- Name of the procedure

- As a processor (yes / no)

- Date of entry

- Name of the person responsible

- E-mail address of the responsible person

- Telephone number of the responsible person

- Description of the processing & purpose

- Affected groups of people

- Affected data

- recipient of the data

- recipient of the data in a third country

- Description of how the data transfer to the third country is secured

- extinguishing time

- Description of the IT security of the data (TOM)

- Description of the physical security of the data (TOM)

1.6. Information Obligation in the GDPR

Much has been in the General Data Protection Regulation since the BDSG and therefore not new. However, the information duty is new this time. With the information requirement you have to inform your users BEFORE processing the data, what you do with these data, as long as you collect them directly from him. If you do NOT receive it directly from the person concerned, but through others, this means then this is definitely to indicate, that is, you must inform the person concerned within 4 weeks about it.

For websites and blogs, this information obligation is usually done by the privacy policy. If you collect and process users' data outside your website, you must inform them. Various and new changes in the GDPR against the BDSG has written down the data protector Regina Stoiber in her blog post[19].

---

[19] Vgl. https://regina-stoiber.com/2018/03/03/informationspflicht-GDPR-bdsg-neu/

1.7. GDPR for mid-size & Enterprise Companies

For larger companies and thus beyond the blogger size, it goes on for most companies even further. Therefore, one had sufficient time (2 years) to deal with this issue and implement the measures discovered. As mentioned earlier, much has remained the same and there are only a few new changes. Most of them have already been available since the German Telemedia Act (TMG) or the Federal Data Protection Act (BDSG) and were still partially not implemented.

For many companies, things continue, and it is important to check what has to be done. As systems and procedures have grown historically, it is important to consider what needs to be changed and what can be changed. Sometimes new systems and procedures have to be established. Here the analysis and the documentation are the alpha and omega. Anyone who has already documented everything well and in a structured manner should have made considerably less effort in the analysis.

1.8. GDPR Penalties

Violations of applicable data protection law have been and are being punished today. At the BDSG, however, these amounted to a maximum of 300,000 euros. With the GDPR much higher penalties are due. Thus, penalties of up to 20 million euros or up to four percent of the worldwide annual turnover can be imposed.

The amount depends on the severity of the violation of the GDPR. The supervisory authorities are obliged to examine the penalties in individual cases and to pronounce them accordingly. Although these should be proportionate, they should also be dissuasive.

Since the GDPR is fully valid from 25.5.2018 and will be applied, it will lack the first time of experience in terms of penalties and their amount, so it may be that initially imposed lower penalties. These will presumably adapt from time to time and will also increase as the courts decide on the various violations and their penalties.

Intentional punishments are probably punished much harder than minor offenses. It is likely to amount to a review of how serious the infringement was, whether it was intentional or not, what sensitive data it concerns, and how many people are affected by it. Here are particularly hard and high punishments quite conceivable, even at the beginning.

Especially with the currently not clearly defined and controversial topics, which have not only the legal, but also the economic effects, will have to wait, regarding to the penalties and whether it is at all an offense. The same is correct for the courts.

Tracking and retargeting in particular is an economic factor that is of great importance to many companies. This not only helps to better identify the target audience, but also presents their products and services, rather than delivering completely inappropriate advertisements that do not add value to anyone.

Also, better customized content can be played as mine finally knows its customer.

Art. 83 of the GDPR provides further information and details on the penalties and their assessment basis.

1.9. GDPR and its Amendments

As mentioned earlier, most of the topics are in various other laws included. Nevertheless, there are some changes with the GDPR, which would be:

1. The amount of penalties changes drastically.

2. In addition, the information obligation has been added. So it is now necessary to explain to the user very exactly which data is used where and how. In addition, the user must now agree BEFORE any processing of this or have the opportunity to decline.

3. The answers to inquiries regarding the use and processing of the data must now be made within one month. This period can be extended if it can be proven that these are special circumstances, for example, too many requests must be answered.

4. Pursuant to Art. 15 GDPR, which regulates the right to information of the persons concerned by the data processing, this person must now be informed about the probable storage duration of the data. In addition, it must be pointed out where the data comes from.

5. Also new is the right to data portability (Article 20 GDPR). This means that individuals have the right to

transfer their personal data from one responsible office to another. Thus, for example, the own profile would need to be exported and imported on a similar platform, with relatively few clicks. So APIs are needed here.

6. Standard in the European Union.

1.10. Coupling Ban

Anyone who has previously given freebies for e-mail addresses, will have to swallow a bit here. For the prohibition of coupling, which is regulated in Art. 7 para. 4 GDPR, there are some restrictions.

The coupling ban in §28 Abs. 3b BDSG says the following:

*"The responsible body shall not make the **conclusion of a contract subject to the consent of the person concerned** pursuant to subsection (3) sentence **1 if the data subject is unable or unreasonable to obtain another access to equivalent contractual services without the consent**. A consent given in such circumstances is ineffective."* [20]

After the coupling ban from the BDSG it means that a newsletter registration must not be linked to an order in the online shop, for example. Therefore, the user must click on the newsletter explicitly to subscribe.

In the coupling ban from the GDPR can be read the following:

---

[20] Vgl. https://dejure.org/gesetze/BDSG/28.html

"In assessing whether the consent has been given voluntarily, account must be taken, to the extent possible, of whether, inter alia, the performance of a contract, including the provision of a service, is subject to consent to the processing of personal data used for the fulfillment of the contract is not required."[21]

1. This is already written differently and a little harder to understand. It states that online gambling or the download of free content, ebook, whitepaper or other things may no longer be linked to subscribing to the newsletter, ie "service against data".

2. Here is the consent for advertising purposes so involuntarily and that is not allowed! How can you solve this?

3. Unpair: The freebie must be able to download without registration in the newsletter. You can obtain the consent and entry in the newsletter in the aftermath.

4. Integration: You can make data processing an advertising purpose as an integral part of the contract. Then it should not be affected by the GDPR. However, the user must be made aware that the consideration is the provision of his data for Advertising purposes.

---

[21] Vgl. https://dejure.org/gesetze/GDPR/7.html

5. Create alternative: You can offer two options. "Whitepaper / eBook for payment" or "Whitepaper / eBook against data". Here the user can then decide for himself how he wants to proceed. [22]

These are conceivable alternatives and possibilities. Of course, it is and remains a conversion killer. Nevertheless, there are ways out. And you can see that this topic may not be clear either.

Finally, the GDPR is intended to give users and their personal data greater protection. You can also see it as a chance, if at the beginning a bit annoying.

1.11. GDPR Written Consent (sample)

By agreeing to the user's data collection, you must be able to prove that you have voluntarily obtained this consent from the user or employee. Here no form is required, so this can be done verbally for some matters.

---

[22] Vgl. https://www.lhr-law.de/magazin/datenschutzrecht/kopplungsverbot-datenschutz-grundverordnung-GDPR

In order to be able to prove the existence of this voluntary consent in the case of the case, it is much easier and more enjoyable in written form. Therefore, below you will find an exemplary pattern for a written informed consent.

The personal data specified in the contract, in particular name, address, telephone number, bank data, which are necessary and necessary for the sole purpose of carrying out the resulting contractual relationship, shall be levied on the basis of statutory entitlements.

Any further use of personal data and the collection of additional information requires the consent of the person concerned. You can voluntarily grant such consent in the following section.

Consent to the use of data for other purposes
If you agree with the following uses, tick them accordingly. If you do not want to give consent, please leave the fields blank.

☐ I agree that _____ (contract partner) sends me information and offers on other financial products for the purpose of Advertising.

☐ I agree that _____ (contract partner) sends me information and offers on other financial products for the purpose of Advertising by e-mail / phone / fax / SMS *. (* if agreed please delete as appropriate)

_____

[Place, date], [signature of the person concerned]

Rights of the person concerned: information, correction, cancellation and blocking, right to object

In accordance with § 34 BDSG you are entitled at any time to ask _____ (contract partner) for comprehensive information on the data stored about your person.

According to § 35 BDSG, you can at any time ask _____ (contract partner) to correct, delete and block individual personal data.

In addition, you can make use of your right of objection at any time without stating any reasons and amend or revoke the given declaration of consent with effect for the future. You can submit the cancellation either by post, by e-mail or by fax to the contracting party. You will incur no other costs than the postage costs or the transmission costs according to the existing base rates.

2. Tracking Tools

If you want to build various websites and earn money with these sites, then you need to know how your users behave on the site. You should know how many users visit your site per day / week / month, which days or times are the strongest days, which resolutions and browsers are used, and from which countries they come.

In addition, it would be nice to know how the users view your page, how long they generally stay, and on which bottom they drop off, just to name a few properties. You may also want to know what has changed with you, in terms of traffic and which subpage is most visited. What are the associated search terms, how the users get to the respective subpage and, above all, where do the users come from?

All these questions are important to identify potential for further optimization and to optimize your conversion rate, thereby increasing your revenue.

To name a few interesting tools:
- Google Analytics
- Matomo

- Yandex metrics

- Mouse Flow

- etracker

I would like to briefly explain some of them later.

2.1. Google Analytics

Google's own tool is called Google Analytics and is free. It is a very powerful tool because the data snake Google collects a lot of information about different websites. And why should you not use this service, which is offered free of charge? For free, because you're not paying in euros, but sending your information about your website, users and their behavior to Google, that's the price.

Of course, Google can already get some information about your page without your help, but some detailed information, such as user behavior, Google cannot find out without you or it is very difficult. In the further course I will go into why this is so and what it means.

To use Google Analytics, you'll need an account with Google and you'll need to sign in to Google Analytics. In this case, you can also use the Google Search Console, which already gives you some free and interesting information. But it's also the first place to go if you want your website to be indexed by Google as quickly as possible and visited by the crawlers. Then you can link Google Analytics with your other services on Google.

If you now have a Google Analytics account, you can make various settings. You can define what the name of the tracking campaign should be, whether you want to track recurring users or not, and whether remarketing should be used or not.

However, this only works if the user is logged in and has agreed to a tracking, ie Browser did not enable the "do not track" feature. User ID can be used to associate users' data with your page usage and interaction with the content. For this you have to create / define a user ID and your tracking code will change as well. Please pay attention to the rules in the data protection law.

You can link Google Analytics to Google Adwords or Google Adsense, so you can better use the data you collect from Google Analytics and other areas. For example, linking Analytics to Adwords can make you translate the audiences already defined in Analytics into Adwords, and use them to create Adwords campaigns. In addition, you can use this for your remarketing purposes.

The analytics metrics such as bounce rate and average session duration can also be used by Analytics in Adwords. And you can import the goals from Analytics into Adwords. This will allow you to better define your Adwords ads and not have to switch between the two tools.

Finally, you need to add an appropriate tracking code (JavaScript) to your website. You can do the implementation of the code manually or via appropriate plugins. The code usually has to be integrated into the header, which is the head of your website. Once you've integrated the code, Google can now begin collecting and processing the various pieces of information.

From now on, various information such as the source website of the user, which browser and which resolution they use, from which channel they come (organic search, Ads, Social Media, Direct or from another website), whether by tablet, smartphone or Computers have come as well as their operating system.

You can see which page visitors came to, how they behaved,

how long they spent on your site, what other subpages they clicked through, and finally where they jumped off. You can define goals so that you can find out when the user has converted and what your conversion rate looks like.

So, Google Analytics is a powerful and free tool that gives you a great deal of support, but in return it wants to have the information about the users of your website. In the end, it's a win-win situation. You can use the tool and improve the user experience with your site, as well as Google.

Google Analytics Privacy Policy

The use of Google Analytics is legally lawful if you meet the requirements of privacy. You have to make sure that the IP addresses are not in clear text, or not completely, but anonymized. Thus, the IP address should not be completely visible, but only the first two to three octets. You also have to sign a contract with Google (CDP).

You must print the contract of use, sign it and send it to Google by mail. Of course, you should include as in all other tracking tools and also in the integration of social media buttons, a note in your imprint that you use Google Analytics for tracking.

Make sure that you comply with the provisions of the GDPR otherwise expensive penalties - up to 4% of the profit or up to 20 million - are due. These are very high penalties and can hit especially the small entrepreneurs, or online marketers strongly. In any case, when using Google Analytics, you should include a corresponding passage in your privacy policy.

You can also enable remarketing on Google Analytics so that users who have visited your page will still be "tracked". Because the possibility that these potential prospects could convert to your customers is usually very high. Again, this is a function of Google Analytics, which, if you use them, must include a note in this regard in your privacy policy.

(**Note**: This section and tips do not constitute legal Advice).

2.2. Piwik (now Matomo)

Piwik has renamed itself and is now called Matomo. It is a free open source software that is an alternative to Google Analytics. With Matomo it is possible to track the activities of the visitors on their own page. So, it is quite possible to find out which visitor visited the page, which browser, which resolution etc. the user has set. Also, the caused actions and the number of actions of the user can be tracked.

For many SEOs and webmasters, it may be of interest, by which search term on which search engine the visitor came on which subpage. Since Google has made some changes, it is no longer clear which keyword the user came to the website. Rather, a "not provided" spent, which is of course not effective. With certain plugins you can extend Matomo but so that you get the search terms displayed here, after which search the user and get to your website.

You can do a lot more with that. You can find this plugin in the Matomo Marketplace and you can purchase the corresponding license. The name would be "Search Engine Keywords Performance".

Of course, the time spent on the page as well as the exit page is interesting. Matomo offers this and many other great features that are essential for a webmaster. In addition, Matomo will be installed on its own web hosting site and will not send data to American companies, such as e.g Google. In order to meet the data protection requirements, the IP address of the visitors can be obfuscated, so that one gets no trouble here.

Matomo is free and offers a lot of what Google Analytics also offers. It is open source and does not send data to foreign companies unless it is installed on its own web server. When new updates from Matomo are pending, you can easily install them using the 1Click mechanism and then be up to date again.

But also, an automatic installation of the updates is configurable. Creating campaigns and defining goals is easy.

With Matomo, you can personalize your dashboard, view real-time capture, define conversion goals, and track conversion rates, just like Google. Matomo is a very powerful tool that can run on your web server and the data is yours and not Google. Of course, you cannot link this data with other tools, unless they offer a corresponding interface.

The design comes close to that of Google Analytics, but is slightly different, but good and clear. If you've used Google Analytics before, then you'll probably be fine with Matomo. It is multi-client capable, which means that you can use it for different websites and define individual goals and configurations for each website. You can also use it on an Android or Apple iOS smartphone.

Install Matomo

To install Matomo you have to download the files from Matomo's website: http://www.Matomo.org/. Once you have done that, you will need to extract the data and transfer it to your web server via an FTP program. Depending on how you want it, you can upload Matomo into a separate directory, which makes sense if you want to use the instance for multiple websites or in the directory of the domain if you only want to use Matomo for this website.

To install the software, you have to navigate to the directory of Matomo. You do this by typing behind your domain "/Matomo", eg. B. deinedomain.de/Matomo. Then follow the steps in the installation wizard.

During installation you will need the name of the database, the user and the associated password.

Configure Matomo

If you have successfully installed Matomo then you can configure it to your liking. First, add your website so your tracking code can be generated.

Then you should insert the tracking code that you see into the template of your theme for tracking to work. Then you can add the widgets to the dashboard that you would like to have to see the information you want. And if you want, you can define the appropriate goals so you can determine your conversion rate.

If you want to use Matomo according to the new GDPR guideline, you should do a little more. The steps below will show you what else you need to do to meet the requirements.

Step 1: Anonymize visitor IPs automatically

By default, IP anonymization is enabled in Matomo (Piwik). This means that Matomo stores in the database any new visitor IP address (IPv4 or IPv6 format) with the last components removed to protect the privacy of the user.

IP anonymization is a great way to protect users with a static IP address because otherwise their browsing history could easily be tracked over several days and even across sites that are tracked on the same Matomo server.

To ensure that you do not store the IP address of the visitor, the personal data (PII), go to Administration -> Privacy to enable IP anonymization and to check if the last 2 or 3 octets of the IP address are masked.

Anonymize Visitors' IP addresses

Anonymize Visitors' IP addresses

⦿ Yes
◯ No

Anonymize the last byte(s) of visitors IP addresses to comply with your local privacy laws/guidelines. Select "Yes" if you want Piwik not to track fully qualified IP-Addresses.

Select how many bytes of the visitors' IPs should be masked.

◯ 1 byte(s) - e.g. 192.168.100.xxx
⦿ 2 byte(s) - e.g. 192.168.xxx.xxx (Recommended)
◯ 3 byte(s) - e.g. 192.xxx.xxx.xxx

Note: Geolocation will have approximately the same results with 1 byte anonymized. With 2 bytes or more, Geolocation will be inaccurate.

Also use the Anonymized IP addresses when enriching visits.

◯ Yes (Recommended for privacy)
⦿ No

Plugins such as Geo Location via IP and Provider improve visitor's metadata. By default these plugins use the anonymized IP addresses. If you select 'No', then the non-anonymized full IP address will be used instead, resulting in less privacy but better data accuracy.

Save

Step 2: Delete old visitor logs

You can configure Matomo to automatically delete your older logs from the database. For privacy reasons, it is recommended to keep the detailed Matomo logs for only 3 to 6 months and to delete older log data.

Deleting old logs has another important advantage: it frees up a lot of space in the database, which in turn slightly increases performance. Thus, a double enrichment.

If you run the automated script as explained in the FAQ, you can safely delete your old history data and still access all historical reports in Matomo.

Step 3: Embed a Web Analytics Disable feature on your website (with an iframe)

On your website, on your existing Privacy Policy page, or on the Privacy Statement page, you can even give your visitors the option to disable the users visiting your site from tracking, which is a GDPR requirement. By default, all visitors to your website are tracked.

If you disagree with the tracking by clicking on the link in the iframe, a cookie "piwik_ignore" is set. All visitors with a cookie piwik_ignore will no longer be tracked. Under Administration -> Privacy you can copy and paste the indicated iframe code.

Step 4: Respect the DoNotTrack preference

Do Not Track is a technology and policy proposal that allows users to opt out of tracking websites they do not visit, including analytics, ad networks, and social platforms.

By default, Matomo respects the user preferences and does not track visitors who have specified "I do not want to be tracked" in their web browsers. For more information about DoNotTrack, visit donottrack.us.[23]

---

[23] Vgl. http://donottrack.us/

You are currently respecting your users Privacy, Bravo!
When users have set their web browser to "I do not want to be tracked" (DoNotTrack is enabled) then Piwik will not track these visits.

> Disable Do Not Track support (not recommended)

> ❶ Do Not Track is a technology and policy proposal that enables users to opt out of tracking by websites they do not visit, including analytics services, advertising networks, and social platforms.

Step 5: Reference to Matomo usage

As a final step, you must include in the privacy policy the notice that you are using Matomo to track visitors and their behavior. You can simply have this created by means of a privacy policy generator.

Matomo Privacy Policy

A big advantage of Matomo is that Matomo can be stored completely on your own server or of the webhosting provider. This means that the data is not stored somewhere else on a server of a third party, but with you. You can activate the IP anonymization - whatever you should - then you will not see the exact IP address, but only the first 3 octets, better even, only the first 2.

Of course, you should like Google Analytics and other tracking tools as well. Include a note in your privacy policy when using social media buttons that you use Matomo for tracking.

(Note: this section and tips do not constitute legal advice).

2.3. eTracker

etracker is not a free software unless you are a private user, because then there is a free, but stripped-down version (light version), which can be used. Otherwise, etracker is available in different versions and packages. Depending on the package, different services are included. In every paid package mouse tracking is included. The basic version costs 19 euros a month, the gold version, which contains app analysis, shop analysis and form analysis, costs 49 euros a month. The largest version (Platinum Edition) also includes the satisfaction analysis and the customer journey analysis.

The price for the Platinum Edition is available on request, as this is adapted to your own ideas and necessary services. Furthermore, there is a targeting suite that allows you to run A / B testing, personalization, conversion rate optimization, etc. Thus, you have everything from one source, professional and powerful and on top of that adapted to your needs.

eTracker offers a lot of features. Among other things, you can also see a scroll and heat map of how visitors interact with your website. You can even watch a live recording of it. There you see, what happens when a user comes to your website, how he behaves then, what he looks at and how long, where the user clicks and when and where he leaves the page again. This can be very interesting and enlightening.

In any case, etracker is compliant with data protection. There is also no internal processing of the data. Furthermore, it is possible to connect Google Adwords campaigns via an interface to include this information in the statistics. Thus, also suitable in times of GDPR.

3. Social Plugins, Tools, Newsletter, AdSense, etc.

If you use social media plugins, then you must also make sure that they work under the new privacy policy and therefore do not send data to the platform before the user can disagree or agree. The simplest method is as described in the checklist to use a plugin that complies with GDPR. Or you simply use links with the corresponding icon instead of the buttons.

This is then also GDPR compliant, since no data is sent to Facebook & Co., but the user has voluntarily and deliberately clicked on the corresponding "button". You must include this use of social media links / buttons in your privacy policy, which is mandatory.

The same applies to any tools you use. If these tools, such as Youtube or Vimeo plugin are used, must also appropriate information in your privacy policy purely. And you still have to ensure that no data is sent to the platform before the user agrees or disagrees. But also check in advance, whether the tools are at all GDPR compliant or not. Because it can quickly lead to a problem. Read here either the documentation of the developer or ask the developer, or manufacturer and let you confirm this in writing, that this tool or plugin is GDPR ready.

Did you install a newsletter on your site? Super, e-mail marketing is good, however, you must also inform your users in this regard that you are offering a newsletter. You have to tell what data is collected and how it is used. In addition, you must also call the appropriate tool and link to their privacy policy / privacy statement, so that interested visitors can read more here.

If you use Google Adsense or Google Adwords, possibly with the Remarketing attitude, this also includes in the privacy policy and the corresponding link to the privacy policy of the provider. With Google and companies, which are outside of the European Union, you must pay particular attention that they also act according to the GDPR and thus are GDPR compliant.

If they are not, it can be a problem for you. Therefore, always carefully check who is this, where the company is located and look for alternatives as far as possible. Adsense and Google Adwords are admittedly having a hard time, but Google will definitely get something here that complies with GDPR.

However, Google is very well known as a data octopus and the privacy advocates for years anyway a thorn in the eye.

Also, with the topic "comments" on your side you should look if possible, that you do not save the IP address. But if you already save it, there must be a reason, such as: Follow-up on insults, obscene comments, etc. Either way, a reference to your privacy policy is necessary here.

Do you participate in an affiliate program of, for example, Amazon? Wonderful, you want to earn some money with your site - or something more - but that too must be in the privacy policy. But that's nothing new, because here it has been known for some time.

More information can be found on the Amazon Privacy page.[24] An appropriate reference, or a template for it, you can find among others at Flegl lawyers and can use it for free.[25]

If you participate in other affiliate programs, so it is currently the case that you need no reference here, except that you should mark the affiliate links accordingly. The affiliate itself mainly sets only banners and links and it is thus usually no data collected and processed, at least on the side of the

---

[24] Vgl. https://www.amazon.de/gp/help/customer/display.html?nodeId=201909010

[25] Vgl. https://www.flegl-rechtsanwaelte.de/muster-datenschutzerklaerung-amazon

affiliate. As long as the banner are picture banner and aren't implemented with a script.

The data is only collected and processed when the visitor has clicked on the corresponding banner or link and thus reaches the provider site. So here is the provider in the obligation and even not even the partner network, as a rule. Of course, it depends on which advertising materials are provided. In the case of JavaScript codes, it may happen that data is collected when the advertisement is implemented and broadcasted.

It is best to do without such JavaScript codes, which in any case only make the page slower and sometimes even cause problems if JavaScript is switched off. Furthermore, you should here from the operator or from the partner network to get you the information and confirm what is collected and how this is processed.

If you use forms, visitors may be able to enter their details such as name and email address. These are personal data and they must be protected. Here you must make sure that you have necessarily activated an SSL encryption. If you have not activated this, you are not allowed to use forms.

When using forms and comments, you should use the plugin "GDPR Compliance", if you use WordPress. This will always allow you to place a check box below the form or the comment field so that the visitor must confirm it before submitting a comment or form entry.

Should you do anything with financial data, say, visitors can buy products or services from you, or even sign contracts, then there are more things to watch out for here. The SSL encryption is clear anyway, but you have to make sure that the IT behind, where the data is stored and processed, that this is also secured.

You then have to provide and document this in your procedure directory under "Technical and Organizational Measures (= TOM)". Also, you are then not only the data controller, but the data processor, since you need the data for these purposes (processing the order, etc.). Information or a note regarding payment transactions are, as you already know, in the privacy policy.

Do you use other plugins that may be integrated with social media and that blur the data? This can be, for example, a chat feature associated with Facebook. Here is very important to make sure that you may prefer to expand this, because Facebook collects a lot of data and the privacy advocates are doing very strong against Facebook, even in the US! Avoid such interfaces, if possible or use GDPR compliant alternatives.

Generally speaking, the visitor must always know what data is collected from him, what happens to his data, and above all, he must have the opportunity to oppose the whole, his data can be viewed, corrected and deleted.

3.1. Youtube

Did you include videos on your website? If not, then you can read or skip this chapter out of interest. If you have Youtube videos involved, then you must also pay attention to a lot. Now it depends on how you have integrated the Youtube videos. Not so long ago there is a possibility to activate an "advanced privacy mode". For this you go on Youtube, take the video you want, click on "share", then on "embed" and scroll down to the very bottom. Then you see the following and put the hook at the place marked in the picture.

☑ Show suggested videos when the video finishes.

☑ Show p

☑ Show vi

When you turn on privacy-enhanced mode, YouTube won't store information about visitors on your website unless they play the video.

☐ Enable privacy-enhanced mode. ⓘ

So, you can insert the video according to the GDPR. But what about all the videos you've already implemented? To go through this one by one and insert the new link would be far too complicated. There are a few possibilities here:

- ○ You do it manually, in fact
- ○ You use plugins
- ○ You search for the old link in the database and replace it with a new one with youtube-nocookie.com (significantly fewer cookies are set here).

The first option is clear and expensive. The second possibility would be different plugins. Such as the plug-in "YouTube Lyte". The plugin not only has the advantage that your videos then comply with the GDPR, but also in terms of loading speed you have an advantage, because it comes from the same developer as the plug-in autoptimize.[26]

---

[26] Vgl. https://de.wordpress.org/plugins/autoptimize/

The plug-in loads the preview image from the Youtube servers. The video itself is not loaded until the user has clicked on the play button. This gives you a compliant 2-click solution. When using the plug-in, the embedded videos (even if it's just a link to the video) are automatically detected and replaced by the compliant solution.

If you want, you can even say in the settings that the preview image will be cached on your server. This can bring further benefits, just in terms of loading speed and no connection to Youtube must be established.

The only challenge is that you need an API key. Here you have to get one at Google first.

Another plugin would be "Embed videos and respect privacy". This plugin is similar to the previous one, with the difference that the plugin loads the thumbnails right from its own server and not from Youtube. For this plugin you should use the latest version, but this is currently only found on Github: https://github.com/michaelzangl/wp-video-embed-privacy

This list is not exhaustive, because there are always new plugins and come to the market.

If you want to do it without a plugin, but do not necessarily want to customize each link manually, then you can go through the database. Very important: **MAKE BACKUP FROM THE DATABASE!**

First of all, you log into your database or phpmyadmin and go to SQL (or alternatively search). For the variant via SQL, you can then enter the following command:

*SELECT * FROM wp_posts WHERE post_content LIKE "%youtube.com%"*

For wp_posts, you may need to use your prefix. If you have "banane_wp_posts", then you take this. Post_content searches the entire content of the database. As a result, you should get something like this:

> ✅ Zeige Datensätze 0 - 24 (59 insgesamt, Die Abfrage dauerte 0.0347 Sekunden.)

Nothing has been changed here, just searched. You can see how many records are now found. In these records, you should now find "youtube.com". You can now look at each record and let it convince you that it's true. Now you can manually edit each record or use the following command:

UPDATE wp_posts SET post_content = REPLACE (post_content, "www.youtube.com/", "www.youtube-nocookie.com/")

Again, replace "wp_posts" with your prefix. This command now goes through all the content and replaces "youtube" with "youtube-nocookie.com". You can also "simulate" the command first. This button can be found next to the "OK" button on the right. It makes sense to have this simulated first.

Also note that it may come with the inclusion of Youtube videos may also come to different variants. It is possible that you also integrated the links as follows:

- https://youtu.be/3ncIljk9Keg (Shortener URL)
- https://www.youtube.com/watch?v=3ncIljk9Keg

Then the command for the first link would have:

UPDATE wp_posts SET post_content = REPLACE (post_content, "www.youtu.be/", "www.youtube-nocookie.com/embed/")

and for the second link:

UPDATE wp_posts SET post_content = REPLACE (post_content, "www.youtube.com/watch?v=", "www.youtube-nocookie.com/embed/")

ring.

Note: no liability is assumed for damages. You act at your own risk.

3.2. WordPress

If you use WordPress, you should definitely have updated to the latest version. Because here you have under Settings now the ability to create an appropriate privacy page. Of course, you can and should use your existing ones here, which you have adjusted for the GDPR.

The new version now also offers the possibility to export or even delete personal data:

To find under tools or tools, if you have it in English.

4. E-Mail-Marketing & GDPR

E-mail marketing is a great way to get your products or services quickly to your husband or wife. Because a large email list can always be used no matter what the rankings in the search engines are. The e-mails will be delivered to the recipients provided the e-mail address is valid and the sender does not end up in the SPAM folder.

And often it says, "the money is in the list". So how can E-Mail lists and e-mail marketing be dealt with at GDPR's time? As can already be seen in the checklist, you have to inform the user that you collect his data and that he may get regular information about it with offers (advertising). He must expressly agree.

Of course, the double-opt-in method is to be applied upon receipt, but that is already true. The user must also be given the right to object, so that he can at any time choose to receive the newsletter if he so wishes.

In addition to the double-opt-in procedure, you must be able to obtain the user's consent. It is important that you can prove when you have received it from the user. In order to receive the consent of the user, you will have to create appropriate checkboxes, which the user can then **voluntarily click**. These **must not be selected by default**! In the checkboxes, you should place the text in a legible form, so that the user knows what he is hooking for and thus gives his consent.

If you have already created a list of e-mail addresses or collected e-mails in a list, then you must also check whether the e-mail addresses listed there have been collected in accordance with the aforementioned provisions. If this is not the case, then you must either obtain this consent or remove the person from your list, including data.

Free downloads as lead generation for newsletter list?

If you create your e-mail list of free downloads and collect leads, then this may be something you may need to worry about again. Whether this is allowed or not, cannot be answered, but it depends on the overlap between the newsletter and the free download, or lead generation measure. If you let freebies make your email list bigger, this should not be an issue and it should be completely OK. It is always important that you point out that the user has also registered for the newsletter X at the same time. Again, it is recommended to work with checkboxes, which the user must also click explicitly.

Tracking still possible with e-mail marketing?

The tracking of CTR and CR is necessary not only for the website and the visitors, but also for the e-mail marketing, as well as the opening rate. This may be done, but only on the premise that the user is advised that such a tracking is performed.

Email marketing with third party solutions

If you're using different third-party solutions for your email marketing, here are some things to keep in mind. First you have to make sure that the solution used is GDPR compliant. This you can usually ask the provider. Furthermore, you must close a contract data processing contract (CDP contract), because the third-party acts as a data processor. You can find these things in the checklist, at the top.

5. GDPR Intern / Employee Data

Most of them rush to the things that are visible from the outside, ie the website, portal or platform. These are things that can be accessed by other people from the Internet and thus outside of your own company. Sure, this is probably the easiest way to check whether the company violates the privacy policy or whether it is GDPR compliant. Especially the companies want to protect themselves against lawyers for warning, which is perfectly legitimate.

However, especially the internal processes must not be forgotten as well as the data of the employees. As a rule, only the data about the employees for which the need exists and which are necessary for the fulfillment of the contract may be stored. These are usually some personal information, such as:

- First name and name
- Date of birth
- Address
- Bank data

- relationship status (married, divorced, single, child or childless)
- Tax ID and Social Security Number
- Qualification (school education, degree, possibly further qualifications)
- Possibly. Contact for emergencies (with the consent of the emergency contact)
- Further data that are absolutely necessary for the fulfillment of your own business purpose in order to be able to perform the work (e.g. driver's license and driver's license number, data from the identity card)

Data like
- Private telephone number
- Private e-mail address
- names of the children
- Names of the (marriage) partners

Children's data and (marriage) partners are in most cases irrelevant to the employer and therefore may not be levied. Also, monitoring of coworkers is not permitted.

In general, the lawfulness of data processing in good faith, transparency, earmarking, data economy, accuracy, integrity and confidentiality of personal data, as well as accountability, must be handled by the employer and its affiliates, but also by the works council or other corporate constitutional bodies that process employee personal information, get noticed.[27]

Thus, it is necessary to check whether the data collected about the employee is indeed needed for business success or not.

Furthermore, it is important to know that the employees also communicate with other employees and possibly also with customers and partners via e-mail. Thus, data is processed here and some form of contract with the employees is necessary.

---

[27] Vgl. https://www.datenschutzbeauftragter-info.de/GDPR-grundsaetze-fuer-die-verarbeitung-personenbezogener-daten/

6. GDPR Tools

When examining the various things regarding GDPR compliance, cookies, etc., it can sometimes be very tedious to approach the whole thing manually. So, it's good to have support from different tools here. Therefore, here are some tools to be listed, which should support you in your implementation work.

Privacy generator

Imprint and privacy generator of e-recht24 in the Premium version: http://bit.ly/e-recht24-premium-acc * It is in German, but you can generate an English version also.

So, you can put together your own imprint and privacy policy and generate it, which is not unimportant.

Ghostery

With Ghostery, you can find out what cookies are set so that you can quickly find out which systems you may need to include in the privacy policy and your processing directory.

Ghostery is just a plugin for your browser: https://www.ghostery.com/

Google Chrome & FireFox

Here you can proceed, as described in chapter 1.1 GDPR checklist, namely on the left on the key / Infosysmbol and there over the Cookies. Detailed procedure see chapter 1.1 GDPR checklist.

Examine the necessity and GDPR compliance of these tools, plugins, etc. If you have identified cookies from plugins or tools that you do not know, you should take a closer look.

7. Conclusion to GDPR

The "new" General Data Protection Regulation is not as new in many places as some people think. There have already been many laws and there were many of these rules already. These were also valid and in force, but the punish this was not so much in the foreground, as it should now proceed with the GDPR policy. And yes, some is still unclear, especially the use of certain tracking tools (Google Analytics), even if there is a GDPR compliant variant, or a CDP contract and the possibility of anonymizing the IP address. Nevertheless, some things are still unclear.

As for the communication and processing of data outside the EU, this is also not yet clear. Sure, the service provider has to recognize the GDPR guidelines and act accordingly, but it is clearly not. Also, whether the EU - US Privacy Shield is sufficient here.

For certain things, one will indeed have to wait and see what the courts decide and what further changes, and concretizations will come out. However, the fact is that the General Data Protection Regulation affects anyone who has anything to do with data by 25 May 2018 at the latest.

And this is not only the data of the website visitors on their own blog, the website or shop, but it goes on and concerns everything that has to do with data processing, including employee data. This is not new. Therefore, every company usually has a data protection instruction every 12 - 24 months and a corresponding passage in the employment contract.

Either way, even if these measures are not pretty and the penalties are dramatic, this step has been partly necessary, considering what headlines have been heard over the past months or years. Too many data scandals, too much glassy human. Of course, data processing and data sharing will be needed to fulfill and use certain services, but the question is, does it have to be that much?

When apps are opened on the smartphone, many require partial access to EVERYTHING and it cannot be, especially for apps where this is questionable. An interesting point will be the one with Whatsapp. In theory, something has to be done here as well.

Because this service requires access to your contacts and sends them to Facebook. If you use Whatsapp purely privately, this is probably OK. But if colleagues and business partners are in your contact list and you use Whatsapp, this is a clear violation of the GDPR[28].

However, this statement from the source is questionable, since websites are supposed to protect exactly all persons and not create a two-class society.

To conclude, keep your eyes open, deal with this issue seriously, as it is not new, meet requirements and, if necessary, get experts and consultants who can help, otherwise it can be expensive. Having the claim to have read this book and to be fit for the GDPR will be fulfilled only partially.

Because most of the time an individual consultation is necessary, because I or even another author does not know your company and your website, so that information and tips individually for you and your company & website cannot be provided 100%. Nevertheless, I hope you have got a good insight into the subject and have been able to extract some important tips and instructions for you.

---

[28]   Vgl.   https://www.GDPRapp.at/2018/01/16/whatsapp-GDPR-kann-das-zusammenpassen/

8. Links: Patterns for Different Types of Businesses / Operations

Here you will find some additional links to the specific requirements for the GDPR as well as some sample directories, directly from the Bavarian State Office for Data Protection Supervision (LDA Bayern).

I hope that one of these links saves you work and is helpful for you.

Doctor's office

- Requirements for medical practices[29]

- Model directory of processing activities for medical practices[30]

Bakery

- Requirements for bakeries[31]

Tourist accommodation

---

[29] Vgl. https://www.lda.bayern.de/media/muster_5_arztpraxis.pdf
[30] Vgl. https://www.lda.bayern.de/media/muster_5_arztpraxis_verzeichnis.pdf
[31] Vgl. https://www.lda.bayern.de/media/muster_10_baeckerei.pdf

- Requirements for tourist accommodation[32]

- Model list of processing activities for tourist accommodation[33]

Retailer

- Requirements for retailers[34]

- Model directory of processing activities for retailers[35]

Cooperative Bank

- Requirements for cooperative banks

Craft business

- Requirements for craft businesses[36]

- Model list of processing activities for craft enterprises[37]

Car repair shop

- Requirements for workshops[38]

- Model list of processing activities for workshops[39]

Online shop

- Requirements for online shops[40]

---

[32] Vgl. Vgl. https://www.lda.bayern.de/media/muster_11_beherbergungsbetrieb.pdf

[33] Vgl. https://www.lda.bayern.de/media/muster_11_beherbergungsbetrieb_verzeichnis.pdf

[34] Vgl. https://www.lda.bayern.de/media/muster_12_einzelhaendler.pdf

[35] Vgl. https://www.lda.bayern.de/media/muster_12_einzelhaendler_verzeichnis.pdf

[36] Vgl. https://www.lda.bayern.de/media/muster_3_handwerksbetrieb.pdf

[37] Vgl. https://www.lda.bayern.de/media/muster_3_handwerksbetrieb_verzeichnis.pdf

[38] Vgl. https://www.lda.bayern.de/media/muster_2_kfz-werkstatt.pdf

[39] Vgl. https://www.lda.bayern.de/media/muster_2_kfz-werkstatt_verzeichnis.pdf

[40] Vgl. https://www.lda.bayern.de/media/muster_9_online-shop.pdf

- Model directory of processing activities for online shops[41]

Production plant

- Requirements for production companies[42]

Tax consultant

- Requirements for accountants[43]

Society

- Requirements for clubs[44]
- Model list of processing activities for clubs[45]

WEG management

- Requirements for WEG administrations[46]
- Model list of processing activities for WEG administrations[47]

For companies with Microsoft cloud services (Office, Windows 10, Azure, Dynamics, O365, Azure SQL, etc.)

- https://www.security-insider.de/GDPR-tools-von-microsoft-helfen-bei-der-rechtskonformen-umsetzung-a-626669/[48]

---

[41] Vgl. https://www.lda.bayern.de/media/muster_9_online-shop_verzeichnis.pdf
[42] Vgl. https://www.lda.bayern.de/media/muster_7_produktionsbetrieb.pdf
[43] Vgl. https://www.lda.bayern.de/media/muster_4_steuerberater.pdf
[44] Vgl. https://www.lda.bayern.de/media/muster_1_verein.pdf
[45] Vgl. https://www.lda.bayern.de/media/muster_1_verein_verzeichnis.pdf
[46] Vgl. https://www.lda.bayern.de/media/muster_6_weg-verwaltung.pdf

[47] Vgl. https://www.lda.bayern.de/media/muster_6_weg-verwaltung_verzeichnis.pdf

9. Links: GDPR Fit Test

Would you like to know if you and your company, as well as your website are ready for the GDPR? You can answer a few questions under the following links, which were created by the Bavarian and the Lower Saxony State Office for Data Protection. This tests are in German, but you can translate them with Google Plugin.

- Bayern LDA (online Tool)[49]
- Lower Saxony LDA for SMEs[50]

You can test your knowledge here and get the answers afterwards. This may help answer some open questions.

---

[49] Vgl. https://www.lda.bayern.de/tool/start.html
[50] Vgl. http://www.lfd.niedersachsen.de/download/124239

Bibliography

amazon. (06. Juli 2017). *amazon.com.* Von
https://www.amazon.de/gp/help/customer/display.html?no
deId=201909010 abgerufen

Amazon.com. (21. 12 2017). *Amazon.com Createspace.* Von
https://www.createspace.com/Products/Book/Royalties.jsp
abgerufen

Bitkom. (30. Mai 2017). *bitkom.org.* Von
https://www.bitkom.org/Bitkom/Publikationen/Das-
Verarbeitungsverzeichnis.html abgerufen

Czernik, A. (13. Mai 2016). *datenschutzbeauftrager.info.* Von
https://www.datenschutzbeauftragter-
info.de/unterschiede-zwischen-datenschutz-
datensicherheit-informationssicherheit-oder-it-sicherheit/
abgerufen

Czernik, A. (16. Mai 2016). *datenschutzbeauftragter-info.de.* Von
https://www.datenschutzbeauftragter-
info.de/unterschiede-zwischen-datenschutz-
datensicherheit-informationssicherheit-oder-it-sicherheit/
abgerufen

Datenschutz, D. (16. Oktober 2013). *datenschutzbeauftragter.info.*
Von https://www.datenschutzbeauftragter-
info.de/personenbezogene-daten-definition-und-praktische-
beispiele/ abgerufen

Datenschutz, D. (29. Mai 2017). *datenschutzbeauftragter-info.de.*
Von https://www.datenschutzbeauftragter-info.de/GDPR-
grundsaetze-fuer-die-verarbeitung-personenbezogener-
daten/ abgerufen

Dehmel, S. (30. Mai 2017). *bitkom.org*. Von
https://www.bitkom.org/Bitkom/Publikationen/Das-
Verarbeitungsverzeichnis.html abgerufen

dejure.org. (02. Mai 2018). *dejure.org*. Von
https://dejure.org/gesetze/GDPR/7.html abgerufen

dejure.org. (02. Mai 2018). *dejure.org*. Von
https://dejure.org/gesetze/BDSG/28.html abgerufen

drupal.org. (01. 01 2018). *drupalcon*. Von https://events.drupal.org/
abgerufen

GDPRapp.at. (16. Januar 2018). *GDPRapp.at*. Von
https://www.GDPRapp.at/2018/01/16/whatsapp-GDPR-
kann-das-zusammenpassen/ abgerufen

e-recht24.de. (14. Februar 2018). *e-recht24.de*. Von https://www.e-
recht24.de/impressum-generator.html abgerufen

flegl-rechtsanwaelte.de. (14. Februar 2018). *flegl-
rechtsanwaelte.de*. Von https://www.flegl-
rechtsanwaelte.de/muster-datenschutzerklaerung-amazon
abgerufen

gesetze-im-internet. (14. Februar 2018). *gesetze-im-internet.de*.
Von https://www.gesetze-im-
internet.de/bdsg_1990/__3.html abgerufen

Hillebrandt, F. (25. März 2018). *blogmojo*. Von
https://www.blogmojo.de/wordpress-plugins-GDPR/
abgerufen

Hillebrandt, F. (23. März 2018). *Blogmojo.de*. Von
https://www.blogmojo.de/wordpress-plugins-GDPR/
abgerufen

Intersoft Consulting. (14. Februar 2018). *GDPR-gesetz.de*. Von
https://GDPR-gesetz.de/ abgerufen

Juris GmbH. (11. April 2018). *Juris GmbH.* Von https://www.gesetze-im-internet.de/bdsg_1990/__3.html abgerufen

Kuhrau, S. (09. März 2010). *bdsg-externer-datenschutzbeauftragter.de.* Von https://www.bdsg-externer-datenschutzbeauftragter.de/datenschutz/was-ist-datenschutz/ abgerufen

Statista. (02. 01 2018). *statista.com.* Von statista.com: https://de.statista.com/statistik/daten/studie/71815/umfrage/nutzung-von-videoplattformen-in-deutschland/ abgerufen

Stoiber, R. (06. April 2018). *blogmojo.de.* Von https://www.blogmojo.de/GDPR-checkliste/ abgerufen

Stoiber, R. (06. April 2018). *Blogmojo.de.* Von https://www.blogmojo.de/GDPR-checkliste/ abgerufen

Stoiber, R. (03. März 2018). *regina-stoiber.com.* Von https://regina-stoiber.com/2018/03/03/informationspflicht-GDPR-bdsg-neu/ abgerufen

Stoiber, R. (11. März 2018). *regina-stoiber.com.* Von https://regina-stoiber.com/2018/03/11/datenschutz-verfahrensverzeichnis-nach-artikel-30-GDPR-mit-muster/ abgerufen

Stoiber, R. (03. März 2018). *regina-stoiber.com.* Von https://regina-stoiber.com/2018/03/03/informationspflicht-GDPR-bdsg-neu/ abgerufen

Strack, T. (17. April 2018). *lhr-law.de.* Von https://www.lhr-law.de/magazin/datenschutzrecht/kopplungsverbot-datenschutz-grundverordnung-GDPR abgerufen

Weck, A. (17. Juli 2015). *t3n.de.* Von https://t3n.de/news/womit-google-meisten-umsatz-macht-624118/ abgerufen

wikipedia. (01. 01 2018). *Wikipedia*. Von
https://de.wikipedia.org/wiki/TYPO3#Gro%C3%9Fe_TYPO3-
CMS-Projekte abgerufen

Wikipedia. (01. 01 2018). *Wikipedia*. Von
https://de.wikipedia.org/wiki/Drupal abgerufen

Did you like the book? I'm happy about your rating, because that really helps me a lot. So I can either improve or appreciate that you have read my book and would like to thank me for your time spent writing this book.

Many Thanks.

Disclaimer

This eBook does not replace professional legal Advice. It is a compilation of information that has been researched as well as from own experiences. This is by no means legal Advice, as this can only be done by a specialist lawyer.

* = Affiliate links (free support for our work)

Disclaimer:

The author reserves the right not to be responsible for the topicality, correctness, completeness or quality of the information provided and other information.

Liability claims against the author, which refer to material or immaterial nature, which were caused by the use or non-use of the information provided or by the use of incorrect and incomplete information, are excluded, unless the part of the car demonstrably intentional or gross negligent fault exists.

All information has been researched by the author with the utmost care and to the best of his knowledge and belief or reflects his own opinion. The content of the book may not suit every reader, and its implementation is at your own risk. There is no guarantee that everything will work exactly the same for every reader. The author and / or publisher can not accept liability for any damages of any kind for any legal reason.

Made in the USA
Middletown, DE
11 September 2018